Taking care of your

GERBILS

A Young Pet Owner's Guide
by Helen Piers

Consulting Editor: Matthew M. Vriends, Ph.D.

All inquiries should be addressed to:
Barron's Educational Series, Inc.
250 Wireless Boulevard
Hauppauge, NY 11788

Library of Congress Catalog Card No. 92-26959

International Standard Book No. 0-8120-1369-7

Library of Congress Cataloging-in-Publication Data
Piers, Helen.
    Taking care of your gerbils / by Helen Piers : consulting editor,
Matthew M. Vriends.—1st ed.
        p.   cm.—(A Young pet owner's guide)
    Includes bibliographical references (p.   ) and index.
    Summary: Includes information on selecting, feeding, and caring
for gerbils with instructions on setting up a cage and breeding and
caring for the young.
    ISBN 0-8120-1369-7
    1. Gerbils as pets—Juvenile literature.   [1. Gerbils as pets.
2. Pets.]   I. Vriends, Matthew M., 1937–   .   II. Title.
III. Series: Piers, Helen. Young pet owner's guide.
SF459.G4P54   1993
636'.93233—dc20
                                    92-26959
                                    CIP
                                    AC

Printed and bound in Hong Kong
3 4 5 6   9 8 7 6 5 4 3 2 1

Contents

Gerbils as pets

A gerbil is mouse-like in shape. It measures about 4 inches (10 cm) (not including its tail). It has large eyes, long back feet and strong back legs, which enable it to jump very high.

Gerbils are lively, busy little animals, and you can spend hours watching them, for they never seem to tire of exploring, digging, and tearing up paper and material for their nests.

They are one of the easiest pets to look after, and if handled gently, soon become very tame, because their natural curiosity quickly overcomes their fear of being handled.

The gerbils kept as pets are Mongolian gerbils. Originally all tawny brown (agouti), now they are bred in different colors – argente, gray, white, golden, and black.

Mongolian gerbils come from desert lands where the climate is very hot and dry. To shelter from the scorching heat, they burrow deep under the ground and rarely venture out into the open until the evening when the sun goes down.

Water and food are scarce in the desert. Gerbils' bodies are adapted to make the most of what little water is to be found, but these little animals have to spend many hours exploring for seeds, roots, insects, and the occasional green plant to eat.

In the wild, gerbils live in colonies, so pet gerbils are happier if kept in pairs. One gerbil on its own is likely to be lonely.

You often see a gerbil standing up, stock still, listening intently. Gerbils have very acute hearing. In the wild, where their predators are mostly snakes and birds, they can pick up the slightest sound of danger in time to leap to safety with the help of their strong back legs.

Pet gerbils do not need to shelter from the sun or find their own food, but they still have the same instincts as wild gerbils. They need plenty of opportunity to dig, burrow, run about, and explore.

The gerbil house

If you keep your gerbils in a tank you can watch them digging and running about in their tunnels.

If the tank is not supplied with a lid, you can make one of ½ inch (1.25 cm) square wire mesh (19 gauge) fixed securely on a wooden frame. This lets in air at the same time as preventing the gerbils from escaping.

Keeping gerbils in a tank

If gerbils are kept in a glass or plastic tank, it can be filled with wood chips (pine or aspen bedding) or a mixture of peat moss, top soil, and straw in which they can burrow and build tunnels and nesting places as they would in the wild. Gerbils get much of the exercise they need digging and burrowing.

A tank needs cleaning less often than a cage. But one disadvantage is that it might be rather heavy if you want to move it to another room, or to a friend's house when you were going on vacation.

Keeping gerbils in a cage

Gerbils are happy living in a cage, though they probably feel a little more at home in a tank. They also need to be let out of a cage more frequently if they are to get enough exercise, and not get bored.

Although it does need more cleaning than a tank, one advantage of a cage is that the gerbils are easier to get out when you want to play with them. They are sometimes hard to persuade out of their burrows in a tank.

How big should the gerbil house be?

Most tanks and cages for sale are about 19 by 9½ and 11¾ inches (48 × 24 cm and 30 cm) deep, but the ideal size would be 26 by 11¾ and 15¾ inches (65 × 30 cm and 40 cm) deep for two or three gerbils.

Remember

- A gerbil cage must be big enough to give the gerbils room to run about and get as much exercise as possible.
- It must be escape-proof, safe from other animals, and well ventilated.
- If you make your own cage, see page 8. The wood inside must be covered with Formica or the gerbils will gnaw their way out. Also, bare wood soaks up urine and harbors germs.

The ideal cage would have a solid back and sides to help the gerbils feel sheltered and safe. But most ready-made cages have bars all around. The gerbils will be happier if you place the cage in a cardboard box with the front cut out.

Things you will need

A glass or plastic tank

Checklist

- tank **or** cage

For a tank
- wood chips
  (pine or aspen
  bedding) **or**
- burrowing mixture:
    peat moss
    top soil (sterilized)
    straw

For a cage
- wood chips (pine or
  aspen)
- nesting box

For both
- nesting materials
- food dishes
- drip-feed water bottle
- food:
    gerbil mix
    vegetables
- small branch or piece
  of hardwood for
  gnawing

You need straw, peat moss and sterilized topsoil to make burrowing mixture. (Buy straw from a pet shop, and peat moss and topsoil in bags from a garden center.)

This is a homemade cage built of 8 mm plywood covered with Formica. The joints are made with glue and panel pins. The front is rigid wire mesh to let in light and air. (For a ready-made cage see page 6)

A nesting box

Wood chips (pine or aspen bedding)

A drip-feed bottle is better than a bowl for water as it keeps the water clean.

Heavy earthenware dishes are best, because they do not get knocked over easily.

Food (see checklist)

A block or a small branch of hardwood

Nesting materials (see also NEVER box)

White paper

Hay

Cotton rags

Cardboard

Never

On the cage floor
Never use wood wool instead of wood chips – the gerbils may get caught in its long strands.

Nesting materials
Never give newspaper – printing ink is poisonous. *Never* cotton wool, knitting wool, or man-made fibers – they can cause a blockage in a gerbil's stomach.

Wood for gnawing
Never give laburnum, azalea, holly, purple thorn-apple, or evergreen wood – they are poisonous. Branches from fruit trees and willow are best.
Never softwood – it splinters too easily.
Never put anything made of thin plastic in with your gerbils. They will chew bits off, which they cannot digest.

Getting ready for your gerbils

You need to get things ready before you go out to buy your gerbils so that you can settle them in comfortably as soon as you get home.

Getting a tank ready

First, wash out the tank with a few drops of mild disinfectant in the water.

Rinse and dry it well.

Prepare the burrowing mixture as shown. You will need equal quantities of peat moss, sterilized topsoil, and straw – measured by handfuls.

When you prepare the burrowing mixture, chop the straw into 2 inch (5 cm) lengths, then mix it with the peat moss and topsoil. You can do this a small amount at a time.

You will need to dampen the mixture slightly, but be very careful. When you squeeze a handful it should just hold together, but not feel wet.

As you prepare it, pack the burrowing mixture into the tank, pressing it down firmly, so that it will not crumble when the gerbils tunnel into it. Pack the mixture into the tank until it is about 4¾ inches (12 cm) from the top. Do not overfill the tank, or the gerbils will shower earth through the lid when they dig.

Then put in the piece of hardwood, and a small pile of nesting materials, which the gerbils will tear up and carry down into their burrow when they make their nest.

The water bottle should be attached to the wire mesh lid. The gerbils must be able to reach the spout, but you will have to watch that it never gets buried in burrowing mixture.

(See the following page for getting a cage ready.)

Never

Gerbils must be kept *indoors – never* in an outdoor shed where it would be too cold. And *never* beside a radiator, in a draft, or by a window that gets direct sunlight. Sun shining on the glass of a tank especially makes it dangerously hot.

Until the gerbils get used to being in a tank, fix pieces of cardboard or thick paper around the outside. Gerbils sometimes hurt themselves by running up hard against the glass walls of a tank because they do not realize the glass is there.

The gerbils are also more likely to dig a tunnel up against the glass if it is covered. When you remove the cardboard in a few days, you can watch the gerbils "underground."

11

Cardboard tubes make good tunnels for the gerbils to run through. You will need to start collecting empty kitchen paper towel and toilet paper rolls, as you will find the gerbils quickly chew them up to use as nesting material.

The nesting box should be about 4¾ by 4¾ inches (12 × 12 cm), and made of hardwood, not thin plastic. A tin box can be used, as long as it has no sharp edges, and will not rust (a small cookie tin, for example – not an empty vegetable or fruit can).

Getting a cage ready

Wash out the cage with a few drops of mild disinfectant in the water.

Rinse and dry it well.

Spread a layer of wood chips – about 1 inch (2 cm) deep – over the floor. Rinse and fill the water bottle with fresh water and fix it on the bars of the cage, well above the wood chips.

Lastly arrange the nesting box in one corner, and put in the wood for gnawing and a pile of nesting materials.

To make sure your gerbils get enough exercise, you can give them a ladder to climb and cardboard tubes to run in and out of. Exercise wheels are not recommended. The gerbils can get their tails caught in the type of wheel with bars, and if it is the solid plastic kind they will nibble it, which is bad for them.

How many gerbils?

Before you buy your gerbils you should decide how many you want to keep, and which sex they should be.

One gerbil kept on its own will be lonely unless you can give it a lot of your time, and have it out to play regularly and often.

One male and one female will live together happily, provided they are put together before they are eight weeks old. Of course they will mate. Gerbils are one of the easier pets to breed, but they *can* have six litters a year and as many as six babies in each litter. So it may be a problem finding homes for the young ones.

Two females (or three if their tank or cage measures 26 by 11¾ inches [65 × 30 cm] or more) are best if you do not want them to breed. But they must come from the same litter or be put together before they are eight weeks old. Sometimes **two males** from the same litter are kept together successfully, but there is a risk that they will fight when grown-up.

Fights among gerbils are rare, and these are usually territorial or between gerbils that are strangers to each other. So it is important to give them enough space to live in, and *never* to put two adult strangers together. Young gerbils play at mock fighting, but this is nothing to worry about.

Take your time and watch the gerbils playing for a while, before choosing the ones you like best.

It is important to choose healthy gerbils. If they are tame enough, and not too frisky, the pet store assistant will show you the ones you like outside the cage.

Buying gerbils

Many pet stores sell gerbils, or friends may know of young ones needing homes.

What age should the gerbils be?
Under twelve weeks is best. If you choose two from different litters, they must be put together before eight weeks old.

Which sex are they?
It shows you on page 31 how to find out which are male gerbils and which female.

Are the gerbils healthy?
Their bodies should be smooth and well-rounded, not bony.

Their coats should be clean and shiny, with no bald patches.

Their eyes should be clean and bright.

Their noses should not be sore or runny.

There should be no dirty fur around the base of their tails – a sign of diarrhea.

What food are the gerbils used to?
Find out what food the gerbils have been eating, so you can give the same. If you want to feed them differently, wait a week or so, and then change to other foods gradually.

Taking your gerbils home
The pet store will give you a cardboard box in which to take your gerbils home. But if your journey will be more than about an hour, take along a small plastic box. It must close securely and have air holes.

It is a mistake to try to play with your gerbils when you first get home. The journey will have been stressful for them, and if you try to pick up or stroke them too soon, they may be frightened and more difficult to handle later. Give them two days to get used to their new home before you begin to tame them.

Taming and handling

Never

Never shout or talk loudly while handling your gerbils.
Never make jerky movements.
Never grip them tightly, or squeeze them.
Never grab them by the tail.

Remember

- Tame and handle your gerbils at the same time every day. Just before feeding time is best.
- Handle them for short times only, but often.
- Be gentle, move slowly, and talk to them quietly all the time.
- Be careful not to drop them – falls are dangerous for gerbils.

Unless they have already been handled a lot as babies, gerbils need careful and patient taming before they will happily let themselves be picked up and played with. You should be able to tame your gerbils in two or three weeks if you follow the method on page 17.

Taming is best begun either in the gerbil house or the safe play space (see page 22), and just before the gerbils' feeding time when they are hungry. Be patient, don't rush them – and don't be afraid they will bite. Gerbils only bite if frightened, usually by being grabbed roughly.

Talk to your gerbils while taming them. They will get to know your voice. Move your hands gently – your hands must seem very large and frightening to such small animals.

When playing with a gerbil, the danger is that it may suddenly jump out of your hands, fall to the floor, and be badly hurt. So, whenever you pick up a gerbil, turn it to face your body, then if it jumps it will land safely – on you.

Another thing to remember is that gerbils are near-sighted. One can easily run off a table and fall, because it did not see the edge in time.

You may be told you can pick up a gerbil by its tail, but *never* do this. If not grasped properly – close to where the tail joins the body – the gerbil may shed the loose skin covering its tail, as it would in the wild to escape a predator.

1 Start by offering your gerbils their favorite food in your fingers. If they are too nervous to take the food, try again in an hour's time. Do this every day until they are running to take the food from you freely.

2 When the gerbils are used to taking food from your fingers, put the food in the palm of your hand. It may be a week or so before a gerbil will eat from your hand, but be patient – hunger and curiosity will soon overcome its fear.

3 Now get your gerbils used to being handled. When one of them comes to your hand for food, scoop it up gently in both hands for a few moments. Think of your hands as supporting it and keeping it safe, rather than clutching it.

4 Let the gerbil run from one hand to the other. You may find it wants to climb up your arm of its own accord. Stroke it gently along its back with one finger, the way the fur grows. *Never* stroke its head.

Feeding 1

Gerbils eat seeds, grains and nuts, vegetables, hay, and a little fruit.

Seeds, grains and nuts

The cereal mix sold in pet stores for gerbils and hamsters will give your gerbil a well-balanced diet of their essential foods.

Vegetables

Both root and green vegetables should be given, always raw.

cereal mix

spinach

parsley

turnips

outside leaves and stalk of cauliflower

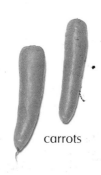

carrots

Some vegetables that are good for your gerbils

You can also give small amounts of cabbage, Brussels sprouts, broccoli, kale, celery, watercress, and lettuce – *but not iceberg lettuce.*

Fruit

Some fruits can be given, in small amounts only. *Never* give citrus fruits, such as oranges.

Vitamins

To make sure your gerbils get the vitamins they need, you can give them special vitamin drops for small animals, sold at pet stores. Brewer's yeast is also good for them and keeps their coats in good condition. You can buy this from the drugstore as tablets, which should be crushed to a powder and a pinch added to the gerbils' food each day.

Give fresh water every day.

tomato

apple

pear

grapes

Some fruits you can give to your gerbils occasionally as a treat

Always make sure your gerbils have fresh water to drink. It is wrong to think they can go without it because they are desert animals. In the desert, gerbils drink the morning dew and find water in water-storing plants. Some gerbils enjoy a drink of milk from time to time, but never let the milk turn sour, and clean the bottle well afterwards.

19

Feeding 2

Hay

If you put in a handful of hay for bedding once a week, the gerbils will eat as much of it as they need.

Wild plants

If you are sure you can recognize them, you can gather some of the wild plants shown below for your gerbils. *But be careful!* Many wild plants are poisonous.

How often should gerbils be fed?

Feed your gerbils once a day in the evening.

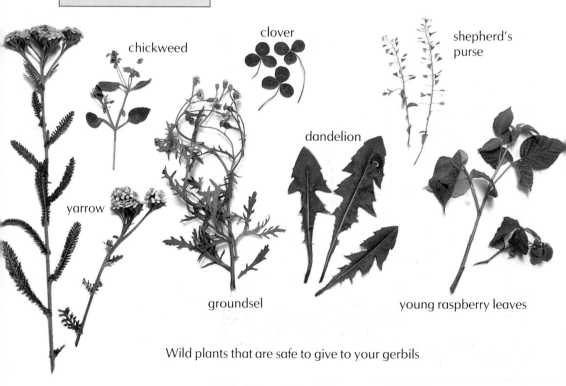

chickweed

clover

shepherd's purse

dandelion

yarrow

groundsel

young raspberry leaves

Wild plants that are safe to give to your gerbils

How much food should they be given?

Give each gerbil one tablespoon of cereal mix a day, and a handful of mixed vegetables three times a week. If food is left uneaten, give less next time. If it is all eaten, you can try giving more. But do not overfeed.

When you go on vacation

If you are going away for more than three days, you must arrange for a friend to feed your gerbils, or inquire if you can board them at a local pet store. For up to three days, it is all right to leave them with enough food to last until you come back.

Never

Never give your gerbils salted nuts, chips, or sweets.
Never give *too many* sunflower seeds.
Never gather wild plants from beside a road, because of pollution, and *never* from a lawn sprayed with insecticides.

Gerbils enjoy raisins, sunflower and melon seeds, and fresh fruit as special treats. But be careful – too many sunflower seeds cause skin troubles.

Exercise and play

Your gerbils should be given a chance to exercise and explore outside their tank or cage, once a day if possible.

It is a good idea to make a safe play space out of hardboard, or screen off a corner of the room. The sides need to be at least 16 inches (40 cm) high or the gerbils will escape over them.

If a gerbil is not yet tame enough to be picked up safely, the best thing is to carry the cage or tank into the play space, open it, and let the gerbil run out when it feels like it. Or place a small cardboard box open in the cage or tank. When the gerbil runs into it you can quickly close the box and carry it with the gerbil inside to the play space.

You can make the play space interesting for the gerbils by putting in branches, cardboard boxes, small rocks, pieces of drainpipe and flower pots for them to explore, as well as wood chips to dig in.

Never frighten an escaping gerbil by chasing and grabbing it. Instead, catch it in a cardboard box. Lay the box on the floor and sooner or later the gerbil will come to explore inside.

If you give your gerbils the run of your room, first make sure it is escape-proof. Gerbils are great escapers. They can easily squeeze through very narrow gaps under doors or between the floor boards.

Make sure there is no electric wiring within reach of the gerbils. If they nibbled it, they might get a shock.

Be especially careful if there is a cat or dog in the house.

One way to capture a lost gerbil is to lean a ladder or strip of wood up against a deep bucket with some food in it. When the gerbil is hungry it smells the food, comes out of hiding, climbs into the bucket, and cannot get out until it is rescued.

Cleaning

A gerbil tank or cage needs very little cleaning, but this must be done regularly, or the gerbils will not be healthy.

Cleaning routine for a tank

Once a day

Take away any leftover food.

Once a week

Using an old spoon or a paint scraper, skim off the top layer (about ¾ inch [2 cm]) of the burrowing mixture, which will have the gerbils' droppings in it. Replace with fresh material. (You can keep a supply of fresh burrowing mixture on hand.) Put in fresh bedding material.

Once in three months

Clear out the tank completely. Wash it with soapy water with a few drops of mild disinfectant added. *Rinse and dry well* before putting in new burrowing mixture and nesting materials.

If the burrowing mixture feels very dry and the gerbils' tunnels seem to be caving in, sprinkle it with a little water, but be careful not to make it too damp.

Cleaning routine for a cage

Once a day

Take away leftover food.

Once a week

Empty out all the wood chips, and replace with fresh wood chips.

Do not throw out the nest, but put in more nesting materials for the gerbils to freshen it up if they want to.

Once a month

Empty out the wood chips, and wash the cage thoroughly with soapy water with a few drops of mild disinfectant added. *Rinse and dry well* before putting in fresh wood chips. This time throw away the old nest and give the gerbils plenty of fresh nesting materials.

If you sweep the dirtied wood chips out onto a piece of newspaper, you can then put them straight on the compost heap or in the trash can.

The top part of the cage makes a good safe place for your gerbils while you are cleaning the tray.

Illness

If your gerbil seems unwell, do not put off taking it to the veterinarian, who will know if it is seriously ill and give it the right treatment.

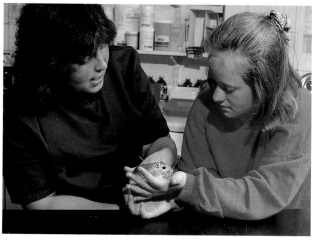

Ask the veterinarian to look at your gerbil's teeth. A gerbil is a rodent (gnawing animal), so its teeth go on growing all its life. If not worn down by constant gnawing on something hard, they may grow so long that it cannot eat.

If well cared for, gerbils are usually very healthy, but even so, they do sometimes get ill.

How does a gerbil show it is ill?

It may not eat. It will sit or lie about, taking no interest in anything around it. It may have diarrhea. Its eyes or nose may be runny.

What to do if a gerbil seems ill

Perhaps it has only got too hot, been handled too much, or is in a state of shock after a fall. But it is better to be on the safe side. So, put out fresh water, make sure the gerbil is in a cool, dark place, and leave it quiet while you telephone your veterinarian for advice.

Gerbils can live to be three or four years old. But, however well looked after, your gerbil may die before this from some illness. Try not to be too upset – the important thing is to know you have given it the very best life you could.

These are some of the more common illnesses a gerbil may suffer from.

Symptoms	Possible cause and what to do
Fur around the tail is dirty, and possibly wet	Your gerbil has *diarrhea*. This may only be a stomach upset, but it could have an infection. So **take it to the veterinarian at once**.
Sneezing, sore eyes, and runny nose	This may be an *allergy*, perhaps to some nesting material, or air freshener. Or it could be a *cold*. Keep the gerbil warm, and if no better the next day, **take it to the veterinarian**.
Bare patches in the fur	This could be caused by *mites* or *mange*, an infection. The veterinarian will advise treatment.
Sores on mouth or nose	**Take the gerbil to the veterinarian.**
Overgrown teeth	If your gerbil's teeth have grown too long, the veterinarian will cut them painlessly.
The gerbil scratches itself continually	Gerbils can catch *fleas* from other pets. You can buy flea spray especially for small animals.
Cuts – the gerbil has cut itself on something sharp	Add a drop of antiseptic to warm water (boiled and allowed to cool), and bathe the cut gently. If the cut is red and inflamed, **take the gerbil to the veterinarian**.
The skin covering the gerbil's tail has been shed, maybe through being held wrongly.	**Take the gerbil to the veterinarian.** He will have to remove most of the tail. A gerbil can live without a tail, but it will not be able to balance so well when sitting up and jumping.

Breeding

Gerbil babies are born without fur, with their eyes still closed, and quite helpless. There are usually four to six babies in a litter.

At first they feed only on their mother's milk and need it often. So never have her out to play for more than half an hour at a time, and make sure she has plenty of water to drink.

If you have a male and a female gerbil you can expect them to mate any time after they are 12 weeks old. Do not worry if you see the male chasing the female around, and drumming his back foot on the ground. This is normal mating behavior.

The mother will be pregnant for 24 days. During that time handle her gently, and give her milk to drink and vegetables every day. But do not make the mistake of overfeeding her.

When gerbils are breeding it is really more satisfactory to keep them in a cage, or a tank with wood chips (a good 4 inches [10 cm] deep) at the bottom. If they are in a tank filled with burrowing mixture the mother will give birth "underground," and it is difficult to know if she and the babies are well.

Gerbils are good parents, and the father will be very protective towards the babies, and help the mother look after them. Do *not* move him to another cage when they are born. If you do, you will never be able to put him back with the mother – even after the babies have gone to new homes – because she will look on him as a stranger and fight him.

When the babies are born, you will hear their piping cries coming from the nest. Do not try to look at them yet. If you alarm the mother, she might attack the babies – her instinctive way of protecting them.

After three days take the parents out of the cage while you look at the babies. Using a small stick, first rubbed in the used wood chips to make it smell familiar to them, move the nesting material aside carefully. If any babies have been born dead, you must remove them, and then put the nest back as you found it.

As soon as the babies are born, start looking for homes for them among your friends, or ask your pet store if they would like them.

The babies should stay with their parents until they are six weeks old. But if the mother has another litter before then and your cage or tank is rather small (less than 19 by 9½ inches [48 × 24 cm]), you can move the older ones to a separate cage, provided they are eating well on adult food.

By two weeks old, the babies have their full coats, and they begin to leave the nest to explore – even before their eyes are open.

At two and a half weeks, the young gerbils' eyes are open, and at three weeks, they begin to eat adult food.

More about gerbils

You will get a lot of fun keeping gerbils as pets. In return, give them the best possible life you can. Remember, they do not have the freedom to come and go as they like and find their own food and nesting places, as in the wild. They depend on you for everything they need.

Useful information

Gerbils can breed at	12 weeks
The mother is pregnant for	24 days
Number of babies in a litter	4 – 12
The babies open their eyes at	2½ weeks
They begin to eat solid food at	3 weeks
Babies can be taken from the mother –	
If another litter has been born at	4 weeks
If not, at	6 weeks
A female gerbil can have babies	
until she is	1½ – 2 years
Life expectancy	3 – 4 years

Further reading

Gerbils, A Complete Pet Owner's Manual
Raymond Gudas
Barron's, Hauppage, New York, 1986

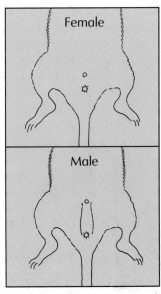

At four weeks, you can find out which sex a gerbil is.

Get a grown-up to help you. The gerbil should be held by the base of its tail, and laid on its back in the palm of the hand. You will see there are two openings near the tail. The one nearest the tail is the anus. In a *female*, the second is very close to the anus. In a *male*, it is farther away and separated by a distinct dark line.

Index